AMERICA AT WAR

WORLD WAR I

JOHN PERRITANO

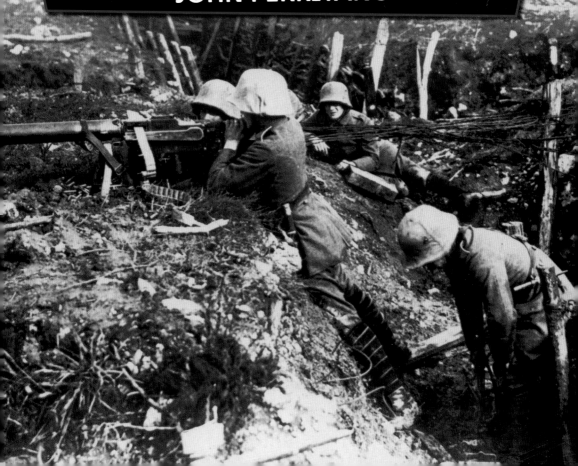

Library of Congress Cataloging-in-Publication Data

Perritano, John.

World War I / John Perritano.

p. cm. — (America at war)

Includes index.

ISBN 0-531-24912-3/978-0-531-24912-3 (pbk.)

1. World War, 1914-1918—Juvenile literature. I. Title.

D522.7.P397 2010

940.4—dc22

2010035049

291910 11/11

Printed in Heshan City, China   62
10 9 8 7 6 5 4

Created by Q2AMedia
www.q2amedia.com

Text, design & illustrations Copyright © Q2AMedia 2011

Editor Jessica Cohn   **Senior Designer** Harleen Mehta
Publishing Director Chester Fisher   **Project Manager** Kunal Mehrotra
Client Service Manager Santosh Vasudevan   **Art Editor** Sujatha Menon
Art Director Joita Das   **Picture Researcher** Debobrata Sen

I WANT YOU
FOR U.S. ARMY
NEAREST RECRUITING STATION

CONTENTS

BATTLEGROUND EUROPE

For centuries, Europe was a battleground for its many nations and rulers. Armies marched across the continent. They destroyed lives and homes.

The fighting was fierce in the late 1700s and early 1800s. That is when Napoleon I came to power in France. Napoleon wanted to rule Europe. An **alliance** of nations lined up to stop him. These nations included Belgium, Britain, the Netherlands, and Prussia.

Battle of Waterloo

On June 18, 1815, the alliance defeated Napoleon at Waterloo. That is a town in Belgium. Nearly 50,000 soldiers from both sides ended up dead or wounded.

Many people were tired of the bloodshed. Representatives of the major nations of Europe met in Austria at the Congress of Vienna in 1814–1815.

They agreed to set up a *balance of power*. The nations signed **treaties** with one another. They promised to help each other in times of war. For decades, Europe was peaceful.

Major Warring Nations:

Central Powers: Austria-Hungary, Germany
Triple Entente (Allies): France, Great Britain, Russia
Other Major Nations: Italy, Turkey, United States, Japan

Leaders:

France: Georges Clemenceau
Germany: Kaiser Wilhelm II
Great Britain: King George V
Russia: Czar Nicholas II
United States: Woodrow Wilson

Top Generals:

Henri-Philippe Petain: France
Paul von Hindenburg: Germany
Douglas Haig: Great Britain
John J. "Black Jack" Pershing: United States

Europe in 1914

NORWAY
SWEDEN
DENMARK
RUSSIA
IRELAND
GERMANY
BRITAIN
HOLLAND
BELGIUM
LUXEMBOURG
AUSTRIA-HUNGARY
SWITZERLAND
FRANCE ITALY ROMANIA
MONTENEGRO BULGARIA
SPAIN
PORTUGAL GREECE TURKEY

Franco-Prussian War

Relations between France and Germany were not good during the 1800s, however. On July 19, 1870, French Emperor Napoleon III declared war on the state of Prussia. That was the largest German state. The Franco-Prussian War lasted 10 months. Prussia won. This shifted the balance of power on the continent.

German Chancellor Otto von Bismarck united Germany's states into one nation. Germany signed treaties with Austria-Hungary. They called their alliance the Central Powers. France formed a **pact** with Russia and Britain. Their pact was known as the Triple Entente.

Both sides distrusted each other. They built stronger armies and navies. They competed for **colonies** in Africa and Asia. The seeds of a greater war were being planted.

Winston Churchill (standing) was the prime minister of ▼ Great Britain.

alliance—partnership

treaties—agreements made by nations

pact—an agreement among people or nations

colonies—settlements in a new country

SPARK OF WAR

Nationalism is being true or loyal to one nation. It is loving one country. Nationalism is also what helped set off the war.

Nationalism was powerful in Austria-Hungary. That nation controlled many areas in Europe. A number of **ethnic** groups in those areas wanted to be free of Austro-Hungarian rule. Serbia and Bosnia were among the nations with people who wanted to break free.

The Fuse Is Lit

Archduke Franz Ferdinand was **heir** to the Austro-Hungarian throne. On June 28, 1914, Ferdinand and his wife visited Sarajevo, Bosnia. The couple rode in an open car down the city's streets. There were shots! A young man named Gavrilo Princip shot and killed them both.

Archduke Ferdinand and his wife, Sophie, are driven through the ◀ streets of Sarajevo.

The duke's accused assassins are brought ▼ before the court.

Alliances

Bosnia and Serbia were near each other. Princip and his helpers had been given weapons by Serbs who wanted to help them. Austria-Hungary declared war on Serbia on July 28. Several treaties went into effect. When Austria-Hungary attacked Serbia, Russia had to come to Serbia's aid. When that happened, Germany had to step in to help Austria-Hungary. Officials worked hard to seek a peaceful end to the fighting. But events were soon out of control.

ethnic—groups that share the same customs, languages, and traits
heir—one who is next in line for property or a title

WAR BEGINS

Serbia and Bosnia are in an area called the Balkans. The unrest in the Balkans caught on elsewhere. The rest of Europe got ready for war.

Each country began moving troops to locations where they could begin attacks. On July 30, 1914, Russia sent troops to help Serbia. Germany then **threatened** Russia with war. France was a friend of Russia. The French began to **mobilize** their army. On July 31, Germany declared war on Russia. Germany declared war on France two days later.

Kaiser Wilhelm II was in charge of Germany. He put the Schlieffen Plan into effect. The plan had been made in 1905, by Count Alfred von Schlieffen. It had been created in case France decided to seek revenge for the Franco-Prussian War.

Schlieffen Plan

Schlieffen's plan was for the German army to move quickly through Belgium. They would surround Paris. Then, they would attack the French from behind. He believed the French would give up in a matter of weeks. Once France was defeated, Germany could attack Russia.

"You will be home before the leaves have fallen from the trees," Wilhelm told his troops.

But the kaiser was wrong. As soon as German troops invaded Belgium, Britain entered the war. By mid-September, the Germans were stuck in France.

Count Alfred von Schlieffen

The Germans enter ▲ a French village not far from Paris.

threatened—showed that harm was on the way
mobilize—get ready for military action

BATTLE OF THE MARNE

The First Battle of the Marne made it clear that the Schlieffen Plan did not work the way that it did on paper.

By the end of August, three German armies were moving toward Paris. German heavy **artillery** destroyed Belgian, British, and French units. The Allied forces retreated. The Germans closed in on Paris, and many people fled. Hundreds of thousands of people left the French capital.

Costly Mistake

The First Battle of the Marne began on September 5. The Germans seemed to have the upper hand. Then, part of the German army left the place where they were supposed to be. They had been told to help surround Paris. Instead they tried to link with another German force. This shift left the German right side open to attack. It was a costly mistake.

Turning Point

The French quickly ripped into the German right flank. The Germans had to shift troops from other locations to help in the fight. This left a 30-mile gap in the center of the German lines. The gap was spotted by Allied planes. The Allied air forces reported about the gap, and British and French soldiers marched into it. They pushed the enemy across the Marne River.

The Germans would not give up. They fought hard. The French line seemed to be falling apart. Then, the French found a way to move in more troops. Six hundred French taxicabs carried 6,000 troops from Paris to the battlefront on September 7. Each cab made several trips. On September 8, the French began a **counterattack.** This created an even bigger hole in the center of the German line. The Allies won the battle.

The Germans had attacked quickly and boldly. Yet, the Allies were able to stop the German **offensive**. The Germans withdrew from the battlefield on September 10. They dug trenches some 40 miles away. This set the scene for the fighting to come.

British troops take their positions at the Battle of the Marne. ▶

artillery—large but moveable guns, such as rockets and cannons
counterattack—an attack made against an enemy's attack
offensive—an attack, or making an attack

TRENCH WARFARE

Before World War I, armies fought in the open. World War I (WWI) changed all that.

WWI armies used heavy artillery. They operated machine guns, tanks, and airplanes. The new weapons changed things. The people in charge had to change their battle **tactics**. Both sides dug trenches deep into the earth. These holes in the ground offered protection for the troops.

No-Man's Land

Soldiers would rise from their ruts and attack head-on through "no-man's land." That was the killing field between the trenches. The trenches were often just a few hundred yards apart. Many men were butchered the moment they climbed out of the earth. Even more died as they crawled on their bellies toward the enemy. **Barbed wire** and **mines** slowed the oncoming troops. But the wires and mines could not stop heavy cannon fire and machine gun rounds.

German soldiers fight from a trench. ▼

Life in the Trenches

The trenches were underground cities. Inside were command posts, where officers mapped out battle plans. Soldiers ate, slept, and relieved themselves in their underground homes. Men were treated for battle wounds in underground hospitals.

The trenches were wet and dirty. Unwelcome visitors made the soldiers' lives even more difficult. Rats ate the skin off the dead. The rodents carried disease to the troops. Lice were also a problem. Soldiers rarely took baths or washed their clothes, which made the problem worse. The lice carried trench fever, a painful disease. Thousands of troops died from sickness and the conditions.

Eastern, Western, and Italian Fronts

North Sea
Baltic Sea
Riga
Berlin
Ypres
GERMANY
Warsaw
③
Vimy
Mons
BELGIUM
Verdun
①
AUSTRIA-HUNGARY
Vienna
SWITZERLAND
②
Budapest
FRANCE
Venice
Trieste
ROMANIA
Adriatic Sea
SERBIA
BULGARIA
ITALY
GREECE

① The Western Front
② The Italian Front
③ The Eastern Front

tactics—plans
barbed wire—wire wrapped with sharp metal edges
mines—buried bombs that explode on contact

WAR AT SEA

World War I was battled in the trenches and fought on the sea.

Both Britain and Germany had powerful navies. Britain's Royal Navy formed a **blockade** against Germany. The British navy stopped all ships. The sailors searched the ships for weapons. They looked for cargo that might help the Germans win the war.

U-Boats

Germany wanted to break the blockade. The Germans began attacking ships from Britain and other nations. The Germans had submarines called U-boats. They used the U-boats to fire **torpedoes** on any ships believed to be bringing supplies to Britain. In time, the Germans were sinking hundreds of supply ships each month.

This drawing shows the Lusitania as it sinks. ▼

U.S. newspapers spread the news of the sinking of the Lusitania. ▶

The New York Times.

LUSITANIA SUNK BY A SUBMARINE, PROBABLY 1,260 DEAD; TWICE TORPEDOED OFF IRISH COAST; SINKS IN 15 MINUTES; CAPT. TURNER SAVED, FROHMAN AND VANDERBILT MISSING; WASHINGTON BELIEVES THAT A GRAVE CRISIS IS AT HAND

Sinking of the *Lusitania*

It was the afternoon of May 7, 1915. A U-boat torpedoed the passenger ship SS *Lusitania*. The ship was about 14 miles off the coast of Ireland. The attack killed 1,200 people, including 128 Americans.

The Germans said the *Lusitania* was a fair target because it carried guns and artillery shells. But the sinking angered many people in the United States, which was still a **neutral** country. U.S. public opinion turned against Germany and the nations that sided with it. President Woodrow Wilson protested the sinking of the ship.

Germany's leaders feared that the U.S. would join the Allies. The Germans stopped firing on merchant ships. They hoped that would keep the U.S. out of the war. Germany continued to target many navy and supply ships, however, in the effort to beat Britain.

blockade—an organized action to stop people or goods from entering or leaving

torpedoes—large underwater bombs

neutral—not taking sides

ITALY ENTERS THE WAR

When war broke out in 1914, Italy was on the side of Germany and Austria-Hungary. That changed.

On May 23, 1915, Italy declared war on Austria-Hungary. The Allies had promised the Italians that they could have Trieste. That is a seaport on the Adriatic Sea. It was part of the Austro-Hungarian Empire. To try to capture the city, the Italians began a series of battles near the Isonzo River. That waterway separated Austria-Hungary from Italy. In May 1916, Austria-Hungary began a battle near the Italian cities of Padua and Venice. This wave of attacks surprised the Italians, who lost thousands more men.

Italy declared war on Germany in August 1916. In May and June of 1917, the Germans helped the Austro-Hungarians against Italy. Over time, about 250,000 Italians were killed or wounded in the Battles of the Isonzo.

▼ *Italian troops cross the Isonzo.*

Battle of Caporetto

On October 24, the Central Powers attacked the Italian army around Caporetto. That was a city near the Austro-Hungarian border. The Italians suffered a huge defeat.

The Italian commander then gathered troops for an attack on the enemy's southern side. Before the Italians could collect their strength, however, the Austro-Hungarians started their own assault. They hit at weak spots in the Italian lines. The fighting ended in early November. By then, the Austro-Hungarians had moved 56 miles. The Italians retreated to a river near Venice.

During the Battle of Caporetto, about 30,000 Italians were killed or wounded. More than 250,000 were taken prisoner. Thousands more **deserted**.

Italian troops retreat after defeat at Caporetto.

deserted—left, abandoned

WEAPONS OF WAR

New technology in World War I made it easier to kill many more people. War was changed forever.

One of the most dangerous new weapons was poison gas. The Germans first used poison gas at the Second Battle of Ypres. On April 22, 1915, French troops noticed a yellow cloud moving toward them. This happened moments after German artillery had fired. The cloud drifted over the French lines. The troops clutched their throats in pain and fell to the ground, gasping for breath. The cloud was chlorine gas. Chlorine can be dangerous. A type of chlorine is used in bleach.

Other gases were also used in World War I battles. "Mustard gas" burned the skin. This gas was also turned into a weapon.

◄ German prisoners carry wounded British soldiers.

An Allied tank plows toward the German line. ▶

War Machines

Armored tanks gave the armies the ability to move through bullets. At its simplest, the tank was a cannon pushed along on thick rubber treads. Various inventors in the late 1800s and early 1900s made tanks into deadly killing machines.

Mass Machine Killing

The machine gun's rapid firepower killed dozens of soldiers in an instant. The first machine guns weighed up to 132 pounds. They had to be set on a base with three legs and operated by six men. They could fire 400 to 600 bullets a minute, as long as the gun barrel did not overheat. As the guns were improved, the number of bullets fired per minute more than doubled.

Flying Machines

World War I airplanes were simple machines. They were often used for spying. The early planes had two wings made out of wood and cloth. As the war dragged on, pilots began dropping hand-held bombs. They also started firing machine guns.

BATTLE OF VERDUN

Verdun was the longest battle of the war. It lasted nearly a year. The ancient city of Verdun, in eastern France, was important to both sides. The Germans knew that capturing Verdun would open the road to Paris.

German General Erich von Falkenhayn had a plan. He figured that if the Germans tried to capture Verdun, the French would send every available soldier. If the city fell, the French might surrender.

On February 21, 1916, the Germans began bombing the city. One million shells rained down on Verdun and its forts for 10 hours. The Germans sent one million men into the battle.

Petain Takes Charge

The great French fort of Douaumont fell after four days. On the fifth day, French Field Marshal Henri-Philippe Petain was ordered to take control. Petain sent the French artillery in new directions. He rested his men by rotating them in and out of the front lines. He opened up a supply route to bring in fresh water, food, and other supplies.

The French front line gets ready for battle at Verdun. ▼

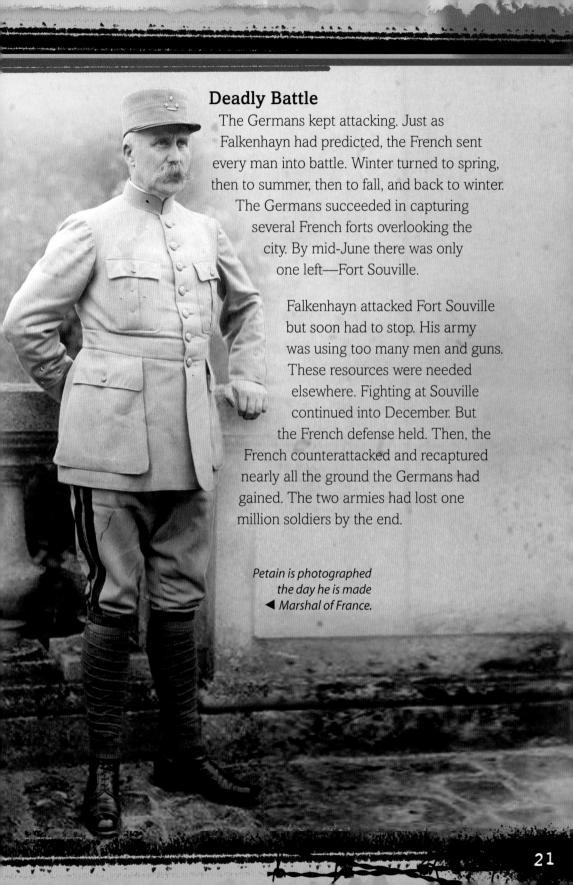

Deadly Battle

The Germans kept attacking. Just as Falkenhayn had predicted, the French sent every man into battle. Winter turned to spring, then to summer, then to fall, and back to winter. The Germans succeeded in capturing several French forts overlooking the city. By mid-June there was only one left—Fort Souville.

Falkenhayn attacked Fort Souville but soon had to stop. His army was using too many men and guns. These resources were needed elsewhere. Fighting at Souville continued into December. But the French defense held. Then, the French counterattacked and recaptured nearly all the ground the Germans had gained. The two armies had lost one million soldiers by the end.

Petain is photographed the day he is made ◄ Marshal of France.

THE BATTLE OF THE SOMME

The Allies tried to take the pressure off the French troops at Verdun. Their strategy was to get the Germans to redirect their forces to other battles.

The Battle of the Somme ▼ rages in August 1916.

The Russians went on the attack in Eastern Europe. On the Western Front, the British and French began an offensive along the Somme River in northern France. The Somme offensive was meant to wear the Germans down, rather than gain territory.

"Duds"

The fighting began on June 24, 1916. British artillery hit German lines. The Germans, however, had been digging trenches and building walls along the Somme since 1914. The shelling did little damage. The artillery did not destroy the concrete **bunkers** that protected German troops. Moreover, many of the 1.5 million British artillery shells were "duds" that did not explode. The Germans were ready, not weak, when the British **infantry** attacked on July 1.

British Tragedy

The Germans put up a strong defense. An estimated 58,000 British soldiers died on the first day of the attack. The two sides fought for many months. In the end, the Battle of the Somme was a big loss for the Allies. By mid-November the offensive was over. The British had lost about 420,000 troops; the French, 200,00; and the Germans, 650,000.

bunkers—underground shelters
infantry—foot soldiers

U.S. ENTERS THE WAR

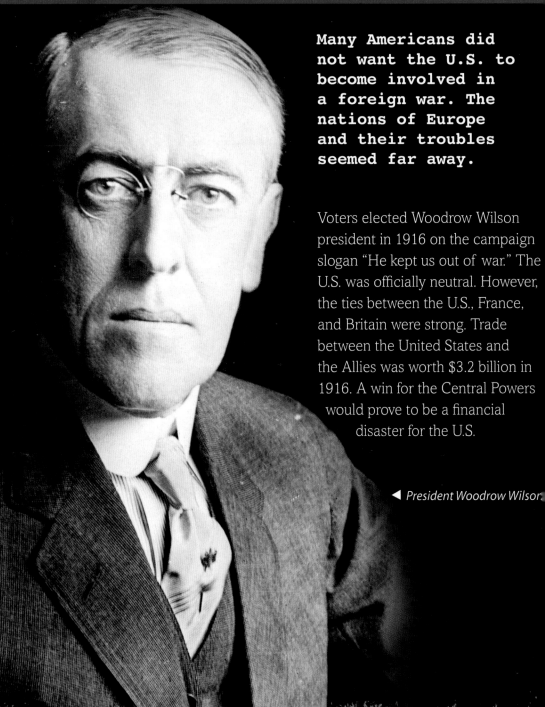

Many Americans did not want the U.S. to become involved in a foreign war. The nations of Europe and their troubles seemed far away.

Voters elected Woodrow Wilson president in 1916 on the campaign slogan "He kept us out of war." The U.S. was officially neutral. However, the ties between the U.S., France, and Britain were strong. Trade between the United States and the Allies was worth $3.2 billion in 1916. A win for the Central Powers would prove to be a financial disaster for the U.S.

◀ *President Woodrow Wilson.*

Headed for War

Wilson tried to make a peace agreement, but was unsuccessful. The situation soon became worse. The Germans announced that they would make more attacks with their U-boats again. Some people in the U.S. began to wonder if the U.S. should fight back.

Zimmermann Telegraph

In February 1917, British officials made a telegram public. The message came from a German official named Arthur Zimmermann. Zimmermann had sent the telegram to the Mexican government. In it, the Germans made a promise. They said that if Mexico joined the war on Germany's side, Mexico could take back territory in the southern United States. Wilson was angry. He asked Congress to go to war with Germany. Congress granted Wilson's request on April 6.

Posters were used to recruit U.S. soldiers.

Over There

The United States was not prepared for war. Its army was small, and its air force was even smaller. The country's navy had never fought in a major battle. Yet, the U.S. quickly started up the American Expeditionary Force (AEF) under General John J. Pershing. The first U.S. troops of the AEF reached the front in France in October 1917.

REVOLUTION IN RUSSIA

In March 1917, an event occurred in Russia that many feared would change the outcome of the war.

Russia's **czar** was Nicholas II. He came to power in 1896. Many people thought the Russian **monarchy** was evil. He did little to fix this problem. He ruled with total power. In 1905, the Russians **revolted** after a war with Japan. Nicholas barely made it through the revolt. By the time World War I began, unrest in Russia had reached its highest point.

Czar Nicholas II

Revolt

Russian losses in WWI added up. The czar's hold on power grew shaky. There were riots and strikes over a lack of food. The country was falling apart. Hundreds of thousands of protesters took to the streets in Petrograd (now St. Petersburg) on February 23 and March 11, 1917. They fought with the police. The revolt spread throughout Russia, ending the czar's rule on March 15. Nicholas left the throne to his brother Michael, who refused the crown.

Lenin Seizes Power

Russian **communists** took control of the government. The Communist Party, led by Vladimir Lenin, took power in November 1917. Lenin formed the first communist state.

Peace Treaty

The new Russian government signed a peace treaty with the Central Powers in March 1918. Russia gave territory to Germany. The land included Ukraine, Finland, and Polish and Baltic areas. The war in the East was over. Germany could give all its attention to the Western Front.

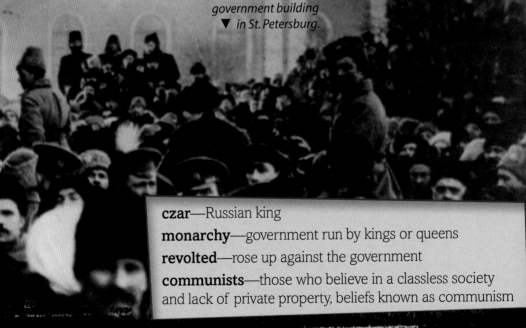

A mob gathers outside a government building ▼ in St. Petersburg.

czar—Russian king

monarchy—government run by kings or queens

revolted—rose up against the government

communists—those who believe in a classless society and lack of private property, beliefs known as communism

GERMANY'S LAST GASP

Russia was out of the war. The full U.S. force was not yet in Europe. That is when Germany made one last push for victory.

German General Erich von Ludendorff planned to take as much territory as possible and then **negotiate** a peace treaty. He began an attack called the Spring Offensive on March 21, 1918.

Over the next four months, the Germans started five major attacks at the Allied lines. Ludendorff sent troopers armed with light machine guns and flamethrowers into battle. German bombings paved the way.

At first, the Germans succeeded. The Allies retreated, giving up plenty of territory. Then, the Americans joined in the battle. The U.S. troops were fresh and ready to fight. By late July, the German offensive had become bogged down. Additional American troops entered the battle.

Moving Forward

The German army was running out of steam. The Allies pushed forward. The Allied troops kept pushing the Germans further back. By mid-July, the Germans were tired. Taking full advantage of this situation, the Allies started their own offensive. On July 18, thousands of Allied troops counter-attacked along the Marne River. The troops were supported by hundreds of tanks, airplanes, and artillery. They pushed the German lines back about 10 miles. They took 6,000 prisoners at the same time. Throughout August, September, and October, the Allies continued to push forward. By early October, the German high command was forced to call a **cease-fire**.

German troops fight near the Somme in 1918. ▼

negotiate—discuss

cease-fire—end of fighting

THE END

World War I ended on November 11, 1918, at 11 o'clock in the morning. At that hour, Germany and the Allies signed an armistice, or truce. This brought the fighting to an end. Details of the peace treaty were worked out at a conference in June 1919. The meeting took place in Versailles, near Paris. The treaty went into full effect on January 10, 1920.

In this train carriage, the armistice was signed. ▼

Major Events

June 28, 1914
Gavrilo Princip assassinates Archduke Franz Ferdinand of Austria-Hungary

July 28, 1914
Austria-Hungary declares war on Serbia

July 30, 1914
Russia moves troops to support Serbia

August 1, 1914
Germany declares war on Russia

August 4, 1914
Britain and France declare war on Germany

August 7, 1914
British troops arrive in France

September 5-10, 1914
Allies halt German advance on the Marne River

May 23, 1915
Italy enters the war on the side of the Allies

February 21, 1916
Battle of Verdun begins

March 2, 1917
Russian Czar Nicholas II gives up his throne

April 6, 1917
U.S. declares war on Germany

November 11, 1918
The war ends

Treaty of Versailles

World War I had killed about 40 million people. The Treaty of Versailles punished Germany for its role in the war. The treaty redrew the map of Europe. Some countries disappeared, and new nations emerged. The treaty also established a League of Nations to settle fights between countries.

Price of Peace

The Allies stripped Germany of its overseas colonies. The war's winners redrew Germany's borders. Alsace-Lorraine, taken by Germany at the end of the Franco-Prussian War, was given back to the French. Poland took control of West Prussia. The treaty forced three million German-speaking people in the Sudetenland to become part of the newly created country of Czechoslovakia.

Sole Responsibility

The Allies forced Germany to accept sole responsibility for the war. They did what was possible to ruin Germany's military. The treaty required Germany to pay $56 billion for damages during the war. The harsh Treaty of Versailles laid the groundwork for another, greater war 21 years later—World War II.

INDEX